Looking at
CANADA

Kathleen Pohl

Gareth Stevens
Publishing

Please visit our web site at: www.garethstevens.com
For a free color catalog describing our list of high-quality books,
call 1-800-542-2595 (USA) or 1-800-387-3178 (Canada).

Library of Congress Cataloging-in-Publication Data

Pohl, Kathleen.
    Looking at Canada / Kathleen Pohl.
        p. cm. — (Looking at countries)
    Includes index.
    ISBN-13: 978-0-8368-8168-4 (lib. bdg.)
    ISBN-13: 978-0-8368-8175-2 (softcover)
    1. Canada—Juvenile literature. I. Title.
    F1008.2   2008
    971—dc22   2007002999

This edition first published in 2008 by
Gareth Stevens Publishing
A Weekly Reader® Company
1 Reader's Digest Road
Pleasantville, NY 10570-7000 USA

Copyright © 2008 by Gareth Stevens, Inc.

Managing editor: Valerie J. Weber
Editor: Barbara Kiely Miller
Art direction: Tammy West
Graphic designer: Dave Kowalski
Photo research: Diane Laska-Swanke
Production: Jessica Yanke

Photo credits: (t=top, b=bottom, l=left, r=right, c=center)
© Barrett & MacKay Photography: cover, 1, 6, 7t, 9, 11 both, 13, 14, 15b, 16, 17t, 18, 19 both, 21 both,
22, 23 both, 24, 25t, 26, 27t; Dave Kowalski/© Gareth Stevens, Inc.: 4l, 5, 31; Ottawa Tourism: 4r;
© B & C Alexander/Arcticphoto.com: 7b, 8, 10, 12b, 15t; © Chris Fairclough/CFW Images: 12t, 17b;
© John Elk III: 20; © Calgary Stampede: 25b; © Mary Kate Denny/PhotoEdit: 27b

Printed in the United States of America

1 2 3 4 5 6 7 8 9 11 10 09 08 07

Contents

Words that appear in the glossary are printed in **boldface** type the first time they occur in the text.

Where Is Canada?

Canada lies in the northern half of the continent of North America. It is a huge country, second only to Russia in size. East to west, Canada stretches from the Atlantic Ocean to the Pacific Ocean! To its north is the Arctic Ocean, and along its southern border lies the United States.

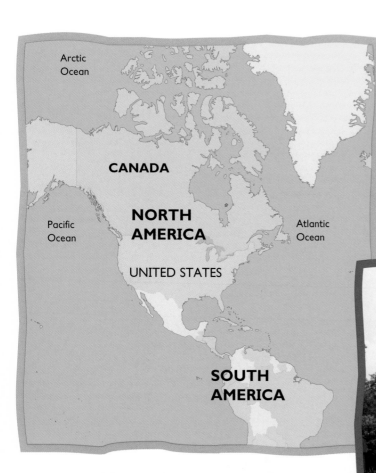

Arctic Ocean

CANADA

NORTH AMERICA

Pacific Ocean

Atlantic Ocean

UNITED STATES

SOUTH AMERICA

Did you know?

In northwest Canada, the Yukon Territory shares a border with Alaska.

The northern edge of Canada includes many tiny islands in the Arctic Ocean.

People enjoy boating and kayaking on the Rideau Canal Waterway in Ottawa.

This map shows all the places that are mentioned in this book.

Canada is made up of ten **provinces** and three **territories**. The country's capital, Ottawa is in the province of Ontario. Ottawa is a city of modern office buildings, historic government buildings, art galleries, museums, and beautiful parks.

Canada is a member of the **British Commonwealth**. Canada was once ruled by Great Britain, but it is now an independent nation.

The Landscape

Canada is a country of many contrasts. It has huge forests, steep mountains, and grassy plains. It also has many lakes, rivers, and islands, as well as the longest coastline in the world. Canada and the United States share four of the five Great Lakes — Superior, Huron, Erie, and Ontario. Hudson Bay, a huge body of water, lies in the eastern half of Canada.

Did you know?

The ground in Canada's far north never thaws and is called permafrost.

Jagged icebergs float off the coast of Newfoundland.

Apple orchards and farms lie along the western coast of Nova Scotia.

The country's richest farmland is found in southern Quebec and Ontario, two of Canada's largest provinces. Canada's central plains, or prairies, have vast grasslands with farms and ranches. In the far west are two towering mountain ranges, the Rocky Mountains and the Coast Mountains.

A polar bear and her cubs cross the ice on Hudson Bay near Churchill, Manitoba. Churchill is known as the polar bear capital of the world.

Most of the year, ice and snow cover Canada's **arctic** north, and no trees grow there. It is home to polar bears, seals, **caribou**, and walrus.

Weather and Seasons

Northern Canada is freezing cold, with temperatures below zero much of the year! In this arctic land of ice and snow, there is almost no daylight in winter.

In southeastern Canada around the Great Lakes, the climate is milder. Most of the people in Canada live in this area. They enjoy mild springs, warm summers, and cool falls.

Did you know?

Sometimes Canada's sky lights up at night with great sheets of light and color. These northern lights can best be seen during Canada's long winter nights.

Churchill, Manitoba, is one of the best places on Earth to view the northern lights.

During summer, wildflowers grow in one of Alberta's many parks. Located in western Alberta, this park is in the Rocky Mountains.

Winters on the central plains in the provinces of Alberta, Saskatchewan, and Manitoba can be very cold and snowy. Summers can be mild to hot, since temperatures vary from north to south.

On the western coast, the province of British Columbia gets a lot of rain. Warm breezes blowing off of the Pacific Ocean help keep temperatures there mild most of the year.

Canadian People

The first people in Canada are believed to have settled there thousands of years ago. Today, small groups of these North American Indians, called First Nations people, live across Canada. About half of them live on reserves, which are areas set aside for them by the government. In the far north live the Inuit peoples, who were once called Eskimos. They have kept their ancient language and many of their customs.

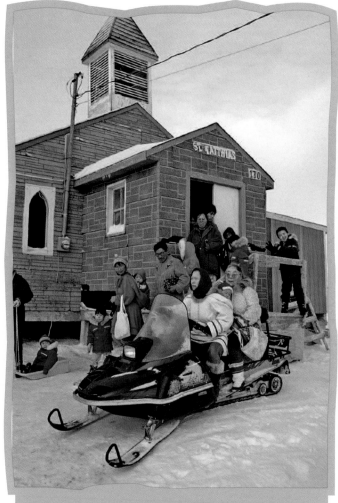

The Inuit once traveled by dogsled in winter, but now many use snowmobiles.

People from Great Britain and France also settled in Canada. Today, about half of Canada's thirty-three million people have British or French **ancestors**. The people in Quebec take special pride in their French background. People from other European countries and from Asia also help make up this **multicultural** nation.

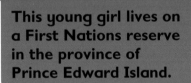

This young girl lives on a First Nations reserve in the province of Prince Edward Island.

Did you know?

English and French are the two official languages of Canada.

Costumed folk dancers perform at a Canadian festival.

Many people in Canada are Roman Catholic. Others are Protestants, but Canada is also home to Jews, Muslims, **Hindus**, and **Buddhists**.

School and Family

Each province and territory in Canada has its own school system. Depending on where they live, children attend school from age six or seven until they are fifteen or sixteen years old.

Classes usually run from 8:30 a.m. to 2:30 p.m., Monday through Friday, from September through mid-June. Children study math, science, French, social studies, music, and art. Some students go on to study at colleges and universities after high school.

Cars wait while children in Montreal, Quebec, cross a busy street on their way to school.

Computers are common in Canadian classrooms. These Inuit children attend school in Igloolik, Nunavut.

Camping is a favorite summer activity on Prince Edward Island. Families enjoy hiking, swimming, and picnicking there.

In many Canadian families, both parents work outside the home. Young children are cared for by grandparents or **nannies** or go to day care centers. Families enjoy sitting down to dinner together and celebrating birthdays and holidays.

Did you know?

The average family in Canada has only three people.

Country Life

Only about one-fifth of all Canadians live in the countryside. Most of them are farmers, ranchers, or fishermen or work in mining or **forestry**.

Families, not big companies, own most farms in Canada. In southern Ontario and Quebec, farmers grow corn, apples, tomatoes, tobacco, and peanuts. Huge modern grain farms and cattle ranches cover the central plains.

More than half of the best farmland in Canada is located in Ontario. Farmers grow feed for their animals, fruits, and other crops.

A Cree Indian woman picks wild cranberries in Quebec.

Did you know?

The early Inuit hunted whales, seals, polar bears, and caribou.

For hundreds of years, families in the tiny coastal villages of Newfoundland and Labrador have fished for a living.

Many of the people who live in small villages along the Atlantic and Pacific coasts are fishermen. The water off the coast of the eastern province of Newfoundland and Labrador is called the Grand Banks. It is one of the best fishing areas in the world.

Nunavut and the Yukon and Northwest Territories in the far north make up one-third of Canada's land. Few people live there, however, because of the very cold climate.

City Life

Most people in Canada live in or near cities in the southern part of the country, where the climate is milder. These large cities are centers for shopping, business, banking, health services, transportation, and the arts. Many downtown areas have enclosed walkways connecting stores, restaurants, and businesses, so people do not have to go outside in bad weather.

Did you know?

About 75 percent of all Canadians live within 100 miles (160 kilometers) of the U.S. border.

The Coast Mountains stand tall behind office and apartment buildings in Vancouver. The city has many beaches along its coast.

Toronto is Canada's largest and fastest growing city. Montreal is Canada's second-largest city and the largest city in the province of Quebec. It is also the world's second-biggest French-speaking city after Paris, France.

Other busy cities include Ottawa, the capital of Canada. Vancouver, British Columbia, is the country's chief port. Most major cities in Canada have international airports and public bus systems, and some have **light rail** systems. Vancouver has trolleys and a ferry service, too!

Ships carry goods to Canadian cities on the Great Lakes.

Canadian Houses

Houses in Canada look a lot like houses in the United States and Europe. Most houses are made of brick or wood and are one, two, or three stories high.

In the cities, many people live in apartments in tall buildings. In the historic French part of Montreal, **row houses** line the streets. They have brightly painted doors, window frames, and flower boxes. Some have upper porches, or balconies, with railings.

These row houses in the historic section of the city of Quebec have many features of French buildings.

In the country, people might live in ranch houses or in two-story farmhouses. In fishing villages in Newfoundland and other coastal provinces, people often live in small, plain wooden houses.

In Nunavut, most Inuit no longer live in igloos made of ice and snow like their ancestors did. Today, they live in small one-story wooden houses with electricity and running water.

Plain wooden houses surround a church in this tiny village on the coast of Quebec.

Pretty painted houses brighten a small fishing village on the southwestern coast of Newfoundland.

Canadian Food

People in Canada eat more beef than any other kind of meat, but they also enjoy chicken, pork, fish, and lamb. Bread, potatoes, and hot soup are popular, too. Ice cream and fruit pies are favorite desserts.

Canadians often eat at both fast-food and fancy restaurants. They enjoy going to restaurants that serve French, Italian, Chinese, or Indian food.

Shoppers can find many kinds of fresh fruits and vegetables in Chinese markets in Vancouver, British Columbia.

Canadians eat fiddlehead ferns made into soups, salads, dips, and pies.

Bakeapples are a treat in Newfoundland, where the tiny orange berries grow in **bogs**.

Different foods are popular in different regions. In the provinces on the Atlantic coast, dulce is a snack made of dried seaweed that people gather along the shore. In the far north, some Inuit still hunt caribou for food as their ancestors did.

Did you know?

Fiddlehead ferns are a specialty of New Brunswick, which is known as the fiddlehead capital of the world!

At Work

Most people in Canada used to hunt, fish, farm, or work in forestry. Today, however, about 75 percent work in the **service industry**. They work in banks, schools, hospitals, government jobs, the arts, and tourism.

Canada is rich in **natural resources**, and some people work in mining or the timber industry. Canada **exports** many wood products, including **newsprint** and lumber. Other major exports include gold, nickel, zinc, aluminum, oil, wheat, and motor vehicles. Many people in Quebec and Ontario work in car factories.

Some kinds of fish are raised on fish farms like this one in Nova Scotia.

Many people in Canada work in high-tech jobs. These workers on Prince Edward Island build aircraft and spacecraft products.

Because about half of Canada's land is covered by forests, logging is a major industry.

Few jobs are found in northern Canada, where the Inuit once made a living by hunting and fishing. Some of these First Nations people now work in **community service** or government jobs.

Having Fun

People in Canada love playing sports and watching them, too! Hockey was invented in Canada and is the country's favorite sport. Canada has professional hockey, baseball, soccer, and football teams. Other popular winter sports include ice skating, skiing, and snowboarding. In summer, people like hiking, biking, swimming, and canoeing.

Did you know?

More different kinds of whales are seen more often in the Bay of Fundy than anywhere else in the world.

Canadians love playing hockey as well as cheering for their favorite teams and players.

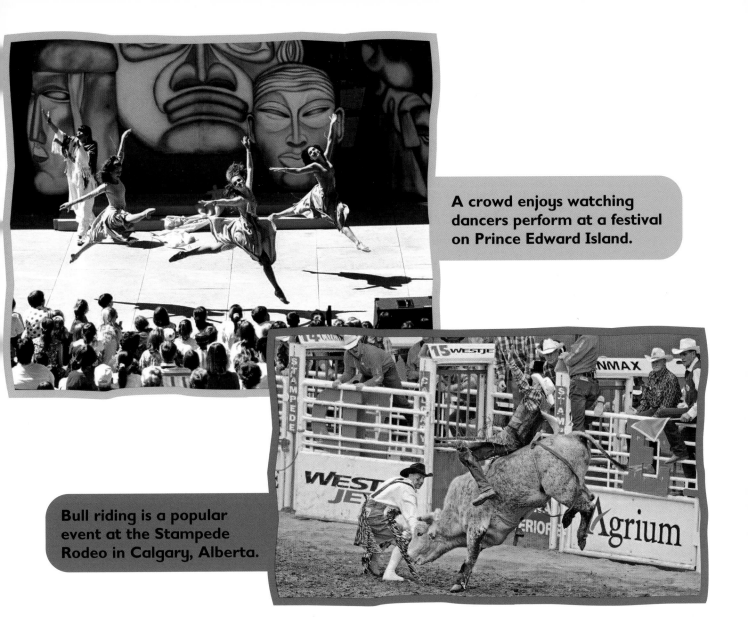

A crowd enjoys watching dancers perform at a festival on Prince Edward Island.

Bull riding is a popular event at the Stampede Rodeo in Calgary, Alberta.

People enjoy visiting Canada's national parks. Two of the most popular are Banff National Park in Alberta and Fundy National Park in the province of New Brunswick.

The arts are also an important part of life in Canada. In almost every city, people go to concerts, movies, ballets, and plays. People also enjoy watching the world's largest **rodeo**, held each year in Calgary, Alberta.

Canada: The Facts

- Canada is a **parliamentary democracy**.

- Canada's **head of state** is the queen or king of Great Britain. The prime minister leads the government in Canada.

- Canada is divided into ten provinces and three territories. Each area has its own government.

- About thirty-three million people live in Canada. Three-fourths of them live in southern Canada.

The Canadian flag is red and white with a red maple leaf in the middle. The maple leaf is the national symbol of Canada.

Tourists enjoy watching whales off the coast of Newfoundland.

Canada's currency is called the dollar. One hundred cents equal one Canadian dollar.

Glossary

ancestors – family members who lived long ago

arctic – referring to the area near the North Pole and its cold climate

bogs – soft land that is soaked with water

British Commonwealth – a group of independent countries that were once ruled by Great Britain and still have ties to it

Buddhists – people who believe in Buddhism, a religion based on the teachings of Buddha, who lived from about 563 to 483 B.C.

caribou – large deer with antlers that are also called reindeer

community service – jobs that help improve communities and the lives of the people living there

exports – sells goods to another region or country. These goods are also called exports.

forestry – the science and work of growing and caring for trees to be harvested for wood and paper products

head of state – the main representative of a country

Hindus – people who practice the Hindu religion

light rail – a system of railway transportation in cities that uses trolley cars

multicultural – made up of groups of people who have different ways of life, beliefs, and arts

nannies – people who care for young children in the children's homes

natural resources – resources found in nature and used by people for industry, including minerals and wood from forests

newsprint – the paper that newspapers are printed on

parliamentary democracy – a government in which the people elect the lawmakers, who then chose the government's top leaders

provinces – divisions within a country that are like the states of the United States

rodeo – a show in which people compete in events such as riding wild horses and roping calves

row houses – a row of houses sharing common side walls

service industry – businesses that serve people as opposed to businesses that make objects

territories – areas belonging to and ruled by a country

Find Out More

Mr. Dowling's Electronic Passport: Canada
www.mrdowling.com/709canada.html

Made in Canada
www.saskschools.ca/~gregory/canada

Enchanted Learning: Zoom School — Canada
www.zoomschool.com/school/Canada

Publisher's note to educators and parents: Our editors have carefully reviewed these Web sites to ensure that they are suitable for children. Many Web sites change frequently, however, and we cannot guarantee that a site's future contents will continue to meet our high standards of quality and educational value. Be advised that children should be closely supervised whenever they access the Internet.

My Map of Canada

Photocopy or trace the map on page 31. Then write in the names of the countries, bodies of water, cities, provinces, and territories listed below. (Look at the map on page 5 if you need help.)

After you have written in the names of all the places, find some crayons and color the map!

Countries
Canada
United States of America

Bodies of Water
Arctic Ocean
Atlantic Ocean
Bay of Fundy
Hudson Bay
Lake Erie
Lake Huron
Lake Ontario
Lake Superior
Pacific Ocean

Provinces and Territories
Alberta
British Columbia
Manitoba
New Brunswick

Newfoundland and Labrador
Northwest Territories
Nova Scotia
Nunavut
Ontario
Prince Edward Island
Quebec
Saskatchewan
Yukon Territory

Cities
Calgary
Churchill
Igloolik
Montreal
Ottawa
Quebec
Toronto
Vancouver

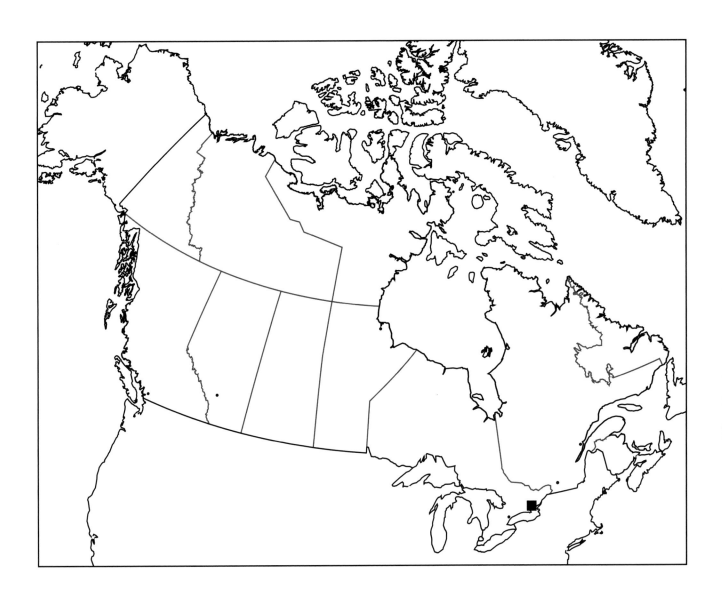

Index